POEMS AND AN ODD SONG

BY

JANETTE VALENTINE

GW00720523

BALANOSTER PRESS
P.O. Box 67, Carlisle CA4 9DE

©

BALANOSTER PRESS
(1990)

ISBN 1 870786 90 4

PRINTED BY
BROWN, SON & FERGUSON, LTD.,
GLASGOW G41 2SG

CONTENTS

ACKNOWLEDGEMENTS

My thanks to Maggie MacDonald for transcribing the music; to Scott Husband for his photographs; to Jackie Powton for her cover illustration from one of the photographs; and Rachel for modelling the Street Dancing; my special thanks to Jimmy Matthews for his kick-start in challenging me to produce a book of poems from my scattered collection of scribblings on envelopes, wrappers and minute books.

Meetings, cursed meetings
Seem such a waste of time,
Unless perchance you doodle,
Or turn your thoughts to rhyme.

THE WISDOM OF AUNT HANNAH

We laughed at Auntie Hannah
When we visited for tea.
She's sit and tell us stories
Of how it used to be.

How gracious were the manners
When young men came to call!
How simple were the pleasures! —
We'd memorise it all.

Couples went out walking
And if Father did approve
Proposals came on bended knee,
Avowing steadfast love.

She'd say that for three marriages
Proposals she'd received.
We always felt how curious
It was this way round perceived.

As years went by and then as I
More wisdom did accrue,
I realised the subtlety
Of what Aunt Hannah knew.

The magic of a union is
Not just how true or fond,
But roles we cast our partners in
And how we then respond.

And as we merge and modify,
Our compromise will mean
That with a different leading man
We play a different scene.

I've changed towards Aunt Hannah now
And pity her no more.
She surely chose her solo role
By knowing well the score.

SHARING

I woke up with my morning pain
And looked around to share.
The cat demanded to be fed
And no one else was there.

So I put on my shoes and coat
And set off down the street,
With secret hope that I could tell
Some kindly friend I'd meet.

My neighbour cried out, "How are you?"
"Well, I'm . . . " — "Here's my bus", she said,
"By Jove, you do look well —
I'm off to visit poor old Fred".

I wandered on at length to meet
The Vicar's outstretched hand.
"Ah, good!" he said. "I've got this problem,
You will understand".

I felt quite humbled as in trust
He let me share his load,
And smiled to hear him whistle
As he set off down the road.

His load, my pain and I set off
To encounter Mrs. Brown:
"I'm limping bad: my arthritis, dear,
It really gets me down".

I helped her with her shopping
And I listened to her tale:
How late the milkman was that day,
What bills were in her mail.

So on it went all day as I
Met with this one and that.
I patted here, I listened there;
Then home to feed the cat.

That evening when beside my bed
I quietly knelt in prayer,
I said, "Dear God, what is the problem
You would like to share?"

He in his Infinite Wisdom said:
"My problem, Daughter, is thee —
Just who in Heaven do you think you are:
My Son Jesus, or Me?"

ITHACA

Legend Isle of thyme and sage,
Whispers of another age,
Ancient myths from mist appear:
Ulysses himself ruled here.

TO COST A DREAM

Time is money, I hear them say.
Money for what? Do tell me, pray.
Just how can you cost to stand and stare,
Or what you'd miss if you were not there,
To summon up a precious thought?
Do they make you pay for a dream just caught?
If you chase the gold at the rainbow's end,
You'll miss the colours' magic blend.
To pot with monetarist fearful tale —
I'm off to sing with the nightingale.

MESSAGE FROM THE SUN

Now look what the earth men and women have done:
With aerosol sprays they have fired at the sun.
The Sun looked down with a tear and a prayer
At the gaping holes in the ozone layer.

"What madness! for though I have power to shed light",
She said, "I can't give them the sense and insight.
To see more of me will at first bring great joy;
Too much of my goodness will surely destroy.

"The poor in the desert will first feel the drought,
Then more luscious pastures will quickly dry out.
The easy-spray lacquers spell long-lasting harm!
Is there anyone down there to sound the alarm?"

US AND THEM

If Us were Them
and Them were Us,
would there still be such a fuss?

If Us and Them at last agreed,
would all frustration be appeased?

If Us and Them walked hand in hand,
would it just be cloud cuckooland?

For who would do the choosing thus?
Are all Them, or are all Us?

This schizophrenic *crème de la crème*:
I'm sometimes Us and I'm sometimes Them.

The truth of all this riddle-me-ree:
It all boils down to Me — and Me.

AFRAID — OF ME?

They said, "Do you know they are fearful of you?"
She said, "Don't be silly, I'm just five feet two".
They explained, "Not the stature, though weighty or
    thin:
It's the strength of conviction which comes from within.

"The radical spirit, forgiven in youth,
Has too much discomfort in middle age truth.
There's less chance the values upheld are outgrown
And more to establish the seeds that are sown.

"If you fire from the heart with an accurate word,
The wound cuts much deeper than done with a sword.
Repairs to the flesh can be valiant and neat.
Revenge from an ego destroyed can be sweet.

"If conscience disturbance is part of your trade,
Do not be surprised at the waves which are made,
So practise survival for the aftermath
When lonely you paddle the sea of their wrath.

"But martyrs are few now, so don't look for fame,
They'll just freeze you out and leave you with no name.
But do not despair that the cause is unknown.
Remember with faith all the seeds you have sown".

POWER BASE OF GOLD

We sat and talked about society,
Of just how alien to them and me
Are values laid upon a base of gold,
Where rich grow richer and more power hold;
Where uncared folk are crushed beneath a pile
Of yuppy fliers in flamboyant style,
Buying shares in companies they owned
While poor subsistence families are loaned
From profits their own industries have made
By Government in money-lending trade;
The strong encouraged and the weak ignored,
As champagne holidays relieve the bored;
While health care which was once renowned worldwide
Declines impoverished like our nation's pride.
O Lord, is it to be a tragedy
That wakens ordinary folk like me,
Or can we find courage for a moral stand
'Gainst monetary madness which has swept this land?
Give us this courage, Lord, before too late
To transform the evil of this greed and hate,
To nurture the finer caring side of man
And bring us anew a bond with Nature's Plan.

PERMISSION

I entered feeling small and frail
And looked around to measure
The strengths of others in the group,
All confidence and pleasure.

I smaller shrank as they discussed
Their management endeavour.
I could not think to contribute
To dialogue so clever.

Until one other's eyes met mine,
Inviting and releasing
The inner turmoil he had sensed,
Imprisoned pain releasing.

One vulnerable soul exposed
Brought forth an instant caring;
But more, it gave permission for
A deeper kind of sharing.

Too soon 'twas time for us to part.
We hugged and thanked each other,
And I departed from the group
More peaceful and much stronger.

MIS-DIRECTED AID

"Now why has old Peggy not come to the Club?
She surely needs the company".
The workers sat round and discussed it at length,
With jargon and intensity.

The one from the Social who visited said:
"It's just since the weather's gone cold.
She says it's her coal fire she has to attend:
She fusses about it, I'm told".

"If that is her problem it's easily solved —
A gas fire we'll just have installed".
They smugly assented, with all but one voice:
"Your insight, I'm frankly appalled!"

"She lives all alone without family or friend.
She has not a dog nor a cat,
But warms to the glow from the fire that she tends —
At least you can leave her with *that*!"

AGE OR WHAT?

I sat at the meeting and thought with a sigh,
"I'm just much too old for this bunkum, am I.
I've been here before: it all comes round again,
Just jargon updated by yuppy young men,
And women who think they've discovered the earth,
With premature wisdom and immature worth.
They view with suspicion my cynical view,
They think I am past it — and much too old, too!
But I want to fly high, in purified air,
Where talkers are doers and theorists rare.
My energy's there when the right thoughts engage —
Perhaps it has little connection with age!"

THE WISDOM OF SILENCE

With all the brash confidence of his young age,
On topics of farming the man did engage,
As they sat around the warm range and sipped tea:
The farmer, his wife, a few others, and he.

He lectured on how and when crops should be sprayed,
And how the foundations of farming are laid;
Of how and which beasts should be fed, and with what,
And why and what prices they're sold and are bought.

The farmer sat puffing his pipe, but naught said;
Just quietly assented by nodding his head.
Encouraged by this the young man carried on.
The wife kept a calm sooth till after they'd gone.

"Ye ken muckle mair than that laddie", she raged.
Then slowly the farmer from pipe disengaged:
"Aye, ah'm a lot smarter than him, I ken fine;
Ah dinna fill his moo by opening mine".

LOST DREAMS

I sat with students in the sixties
Listening to their dreams,
Of love and peace and food for all —
How long ago it seems! —

That we held hands across the world,
And faith from shore to shore,
Combined in ocean strength, to stem
The tide of Vietnam war.

What hope of futures free from fear
And hunger did we keep,
While lullabies of "We shall overcome"
Sent babes to sleep!

And now we've wakened from our dreams
And babes have grown to find
A world of plagues, of want and war,
Injustice of all kind.

God, did I let those children down? —
That black boy on TV,
That while I sit in comfort
Let his hungry eyes haunt me?

Did I not keep a watch on those
Who thrive on human prey?
What principles of equal truth
And love did I betray?

WHO?

Who talks of love,
Who talks of care,
Who heeds the needs of others?
Who wants to share,
Who wants to spare
Their sisters and their brothers?

THEY

They stand apart
And look to be
Out-dated and out-moded.
With heavy hearts
They grieve to see
Their values now eroded.

    Who are they? They're everywhere.
    They are Yesterday's People.

Honour your partner for life's dance:
Do-si-do and take your chance.

SMOTHER LOVE

An anxious mother loves her son
And thinks he's someone special.
She fears he meets a Pagan or
A Red or Homosexual.
Her prejudices will secure
And succour his young life.
The facts of this she'll shield him from
And cushion him from strife.
She fears his teacher may be gay,
His parson could be queer,
The young girl with the sly intent —
The apron strings draw near,
Her female influence all supreme:
And with the best intention
Will offer to the world a man —
How fit to cope? . . . Just question.

A LIGHT GOODBYE

I lifted my toothbrush,
My hair spray and comb;
Without much ado
I soon would be gone.

Six years of together
And not much to take.
The load which was heavy
Was only heartache.

He watched me in silence,
A cold empty stare,
Until I suggested
I take my old chair.

How dare I? he raged,
Did I not have a care
To notice his *Mother*
Was sitting right there.

She cast me some guilt
And vacated the throne,
But still in possession
Of her only son.

I backed out with pride
And a hasty goodbye:
"I hope that you both
Will be happy", said I.

DON'T BLAME ME

I sensed that the atmosphere was under strain;
My friends to each other were cold.
I took one aside and said, "Dear, it's in vain
To waste time while each hour we grow old".

"It's really quite negative: surely your diff'rences
You can accept and agree".
She said, "It's not really as simple as that —
It's *her* that's not talking to *me!*"

RELATED?

They had a little problem:
Who or why or whether.
She said, "It's our relationship:
We must work more together".

He yelled out with impatience:
"You don't half talk garbage.
We don't have a relationship —
What we have's a marriage!"

DO IT YOURSELF

My husband was so into Do-it-yourself,
I learned through the years that it's true,
That painting and plumbing's a matter of practice;
There's nothing yourself cannot do.

I now look around the old homestead with pride:
Jobs done at a fraction of cost;
A wall knocked down here, another built there;
A patio and pond we boast.

I'll always be grateful to him that he saw,
That first time when I asked for a shelf,
The full satisfaction in store just for me,
As he answered, "Well, Do it Yourself".

REVISION OF LABOUR

My husband was useless at home craft of all kind
And practised the art to perfection
Till painful acquiring of these skills for me
Was easier than the objection.

Well, "Give me the child till he's five", so they say,
"And that is the man who will follow",
So why can't all mothers take heed of the need
To house-train the spouse of tomorrow?

And so as I cradled my sons I did promise
That while I attended their growing,
I'd help them with carpentry, painting and cleaning
And also with cooking and sewing.

The years have since passed and my sons, now
    accomplished
And strong, are no more in my keeping.
With some satisfaction I view the rewards
That their partners, my sisters, are reaping.

PROCRASTINATION

'I'll do it when my children grow,
I'll do it when I'm older,
I'll work at feeling confident
And do it when I'm bolder.
I'd like to take the plunge right now,
But I am not quite ready,
I'll do it when the time is right
And world affairs more steady'.
Till now, when I've no one to blame;
The nest is good and empty.
What were those strange ambitions
Through the years I've had in plenty?
Alas, I have no energy
And little inspiration.
What have I lost, what have I gained
With such procrastination?

SISTERLY LOVE

The Dinner Party was all set
With candles, crystal glowing.
In token circle women sat,
The wine and friendship flowing.

We talked of birth and grannyhood
And then, our hostess toasting,
We egged her on to tell more of
The grandson she was boasting.

The topic changed: they talked of death
In detail and unceasing,
Quite unaware that I grew quiet,
Into myself retreating.

"Cancer", "Cancer", on they went
Round and round the table.
"The body was still warm", she said.
To eat I was unable.

Into my private grief they marched
With powerful invasion;
My silent signals of despair
Turned in by blunt evasion.

Then from the party I withdrew
In dignified endeavour.
The cool night air released my pain,
My tears flowed like a river.

'Twas not just for my Sister, though
For her I'm newly grieving,
But that my loss and pain 'the sisters'
Were quite unperceiving.

Oh, we have far to go in how
We love and comfort others,
Before we fly our standards high
And take to task our brothers.

A DANCE FOR JUDITH

'Come, would you care to dance with me?' —
It sounded so inviting,
To let him lead me through the steps,
The rhythm so inviting.

In waltz and quickstep, to and fro,
We two so close together,
In tandem tangoed dawn to dusk
Like it would last for ever.

And though at time the artistic view
I felt I'd like to alter,
And on occasion take the lead,
We spared no time to falter.

Till then, as seasons changed, the theme
And the interpretation
Brought conflict, quite sufficient deep
To partnership cessation.

At first, though solo dancing steps
With nervous grief were tempered,
My independence to make choice
And change became most treasured.

Now partnership I welcome, yet
With confidence declare it,
That being One, Alone, At Peace,
Deserves a higher merit.

NEARLY!

The Secretary of the Womens Group
Had come to tea.
The baby dolls had all been hidden
Under the settee.
The Mother brought the logs and coal,
The Father cut the cake;
Well practised in their changing roles,
No error would they make.
"What do you want from Santa Claus?"
The little girl was asked,
And she in childlike innocence
Replied quite unabashed:
"I want an iron and ironing board —
Then I'll be all grown up!"
The Father's trembling hand his white
And anguished face did cup.
The Secretary curled her lip,
It really was too bad. —
The little girl continued, "Then
I'll be just like my Dad!"

AN IRRITATING HABIT

The platform of speakers was heavily biassed
With males, who were prattling away:
'You'd think that more women would be up there with
    them —
We're supposed to be equal today'.

"We won't get equality", said a smart lady,
"Though talented, fluent and funny,
Until we can stand up with arrogant posture
And jingle a pocket of money".

A SORRY EPITAPH

I knew that man in many ways,
Bible terms and other;
First childhood friend, companion, then
A husband and a lover.
We had of course our ups and downs,
Our times of joy and worry,
But never once in all those years
Did ever he say, "Sorry".

It was not that he was a saint;
More often like a sinner.
But it was someone else to blame
When he was late for dinner.
And even when the parting came
To end our mutual story,
Though there was sadness in his eyes,
He could not utter, "Sorry".

His epitaph I file now, till
The time's right to be quoted:
"Here lies a man of many words,
For wit and humour noted;
A friend and raconteur we mourn
Of first class category;
But do not grieve too long, for he
At least will not be sorry".

WHY AGAIN?

Oh Lord, I've trod this path before,
I know the turnings and the score.
It seems a respite I've not earned:
Is it the lessons I've not learned?

Or is it that you do intend
This time I walk it with a friend?
Then tell me, is it all in vain,
If only I bear all the pain?

DARTS

Many beasts have drawn my blood,
Mosquitoes, wasps and fleas,
But only those of human kind
Have brought me to my knees.

     *   *   *   *   *

Is her talent being nasty
Quite natural, I ask?
Or the practice for perfection
Now her major task?

     *   *   *   *   *

You are a giver to a fault.
I wish you could believe
That there are many times when it's
More generous to receive.

     *   *   *   *   *

Many flowers have shaped his grace,
Many formed his fashion,
Geared his laughter and his tears —
But I have had his passion.

Songs

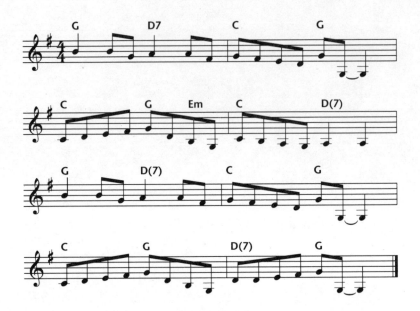

I had a young man, I loved him very dearly.
He looked at me with eyes so blue and said most sincerely:
"Though you touch my soul and in love with you I'm
    falling,
I must be off to don the cloth: the priesthood is a-calling".

When my heart was mended I met another fellow.
I was glad when I found he had an outlook much more
    secular.
But for all my romance, alone I had to frolic —
I hardly ever saw the man: he was a work-aholic.

Then I met a sensual man who gave my life more
    meaning.
He was tall and bearded and he set my senses reeling.
But for all his passion, and I knew there was no other,
He said he'd never marry me — he could not leave his
    mother.

Then as I grew older, my ambitions unaffected,
I met a man so full of charm I honoured and respected.
But he was married, she was called Susannah.
He said he'd leave his wife for me, but not his grand
    piana.

Now as my life nears its end and I remain unmarried,
I have had my moments, but alone I've often tarried.
So if you're a gambling man, the odds are running level:
Who will it be who'll reject me — Saint Peter or the
    Devil?

THE 45 RETREAT

White cockades flutter like ghosts of soft thisteldown,
From Moor of Culloden down through the Great Glen,
To where tall trees which once graced the forests of Rannoch
Lie embered with flesh of the Jacobite men.

They came from the Islands, they came from the
    Highlands.
Some followed a dream, some came by command;
A people still scarred by an unequal union,
Who wished faith and freedom restored to their land.

What courage it takes to face an oppressor,
To carry a weapon and in battle be slain,
To be butchered and hunted in harsh retribution,
Hanged by a rope or consumed by a flame.

But what of the courage it takes of the living?
The women alone in their anguish and pain,
Who father the children and plant the next harvest
And help to re-build a Nation again?

A PRINCE OF PROMISE

Tune Traditional

A Prince he came a-riding by.
He said, "For you I'd surely die.
A lovers knot with you I'd tie" —
    Not so long ago.

He said: "Put on your party gown.
We'll go down to London Town,
And I will show you all around" —
    Not so long ago

"And then we'll sail across the sea
The wonders of the world to see;
A wonderful life for you and me" —
    Not so long ago.

How could a girl say No to this:
A promised life so full of bliss?
I sealed my answer with a kiss —
    Not so long ago.

(Change of tune)

Now I sit by the fire and dream
And conjure up the scene
Of how it all might have been
If just one little word he did mean.

For we sit by the telly and gog,
Just me and him and the dog,
With a bucket of coal and a log,
For — my Prince has turned into a FROG

THE FLU

Someone's filled ma wellies wae tons and tons o' lead.
I'm sore all over and there's hammers in ma head.
Ma temperature is soarin' though I am shiverin' through,
For I've gone an' caught another dose of flu'.

In 1967 when the Asians sent us theirs,
I was struck down suddenly and started sayin' ma
    prayers.
I thought that I was dying, I was paralysed right through.
The doctor called, examined me and said, "It's only flu'.

Each successive year as the bugs have been and went,
Hours and hours of agony in my bed I've spent.
For one so fit and healthy, I am telling you,
The only time that I'm off work is with the rotten flu.

So nowadays when I hear there's a virus on the go,
I get out my white hankie and I wave it to and fro,
Yelling, "Come out, all you flu bugs. I'll go quietly sick.
"Don't postpone the agony — just get it over quick!"

I believe in fairies, pixies, gnomes as well,
Wishing bones and mistletoe to weave a magic spell.
And so on Christmas Eve I'll send a letter up the lum
Addressed to dear old Santa Claus, asking him to come:

    Oh, Mr. Santa, come and visit me.
    Leave a nice wee present underneath the Christmas
      Tree.

I've watched all the telly ads for Lentheric Finesse,
For Babycham and chocolates, computer games and
    chess.
Diamond rings and curling tongs are not what I would
    choose;
I only want a hand to help me light my Christmas fuse:

    So, Mr. Santa, help me if you can —
    All I want for Christmas is an Action Man.

A WORLD OF PLENTY AND GREED

There's enough in this world for everybody's need,
But there certainly is not enough for everybody's greed,
So suffer little children to hunger and to die,
While we sit analysing, asking reasons why.

So many many people have not sufficient food,
And many many millions more do not eat what they
    should,
And there's many kinds of hunger that you can seek and
    find,
There's hunger of the spirit and there's hunger of the
    mind.

So much of this world's harvest is lost through food and
    drought.
The locusts plunder and grow fat while people do
    without,

And human locusts also prey on those whose needs are
    most,
And much of aid and harvest in corruption will be lost.

There's enough in this world for everybody's need,
But there certainly is not enough for everybody's greed,
So suffer little children to hunger and to die,
While we sit analysing, asking reasons why.

DINNA ROCK THE BOAT

From the time that I was young,
I looked around to see
All the sorrows in the world
And the inequality.
In simple childhood innocence
I voiced that this was wrong,
But I was taught to ask not why
And to heed this little song.

Dinna rock the boat, lassie,
Dinna rock the boat,
For all is well
We want no swell,
So be sure don't rock the boat.

But still in work and play I questioned
As I've gone through life,
As I've witnessed all the poverty,
The cruelty and strife.
I thought of folk like Shaftesbury
And Wilberforce of yore:
If the establishment had silenced them,
Our burdens would be more.

So rock rock the boat, lassie,
Rock rock the boat,
For all's not well,
We need that swell,
So be proud to rock the boat.

BONNIE WEE STOTTER

To the tune "Bee Baw Babbity" (Traditional)

Ma Daddy says when I was wee
I used to sit upon his knee.
I'd cuddle in and he'd tell me
That I was a bonny wee stotter.

Then I grew up and curled my hair.
My Daddy said, "You're lookin' rare —
You'll find a lad your life to share,
For you're a bonny wee stotter".

So now I'm trying all I can
To find myself a handsome man
Who like my Dad will think I am
His own bonny wee stotter.

Though family you cannot choose,
Not one of mine would I refuse.

FOR EVERYTHING THERE IS A SEASON

It is not time, oh foolish trees;
Be tempted not by winter's tease,
To bare your leaves, young, fresh and green,
To hidden storms as yet unseen,
Nor blossom out to scent the air,
While lurking frosts plot blunt despair.

The rhythm and rhyme of nature's plan,
Though interfered a deal by man,
By Greater Power was set sublime,
That every season has its time;
And winter's healing resting state
Allows some chance to contemplate,
To anchor deeper firmer roots,
In time to send out strong green shoots.

So nature's patience man must learn,
And spells of resting state discern,
That energy and thought well spent,
Through winters of great discontent,
Will feed the roots to take the strain
Of visions blossoming again.

Eternal hope springs that their worth,
Like nature's vision, spans the earth.

CASTLES IN THE SAND

The little girl worked hard for hours
To build her castle in the sand,
With care and patience laboured on;
The edifice rose fine and grand.

Folk came and went throughout the day
And smiled and nodded their assent,
While other children gazed in awe.
The girl worked on with great intent,

Engrossed in detail, till at last
Complete, she paused to view with pride;
She felt a respite she had earned.
Alas she reckoned not the tide.

The water lapped her aching legs
The shock and cold reached to her heart.
A gentle wave the castle reached;
First line defences fell apart.

In helpless rage she baled the moat,
Rebuilding with a frantic zeal;
Yet came another rolling on.
She faced the ocean with appeal:

"Please turn back here, you cannot mean
My hard endeavour brought to ruin".
The waves retreated, leaving calm,
And battlements with seaweed strewn.

With Neptune faith she faced the task
Of re-creating what she could.
Meantime the tide was gathering strength
To make its assault as it would.

Her Granny came to comfort her,
So cold and wet and in despair.
She pointed to the rising tide
And cried, "I built a castle there".

Her Granny said, "Well, all we do
Can't be forever, or we'd find
No room to build another dream,
Nor fort, or house of any kind.

"And think the pleasure that you've given
To all the folk who watched today.
They've taken home some happy thoughts,
The tide can not take those away.

"Come now, let's dry those salty tears,
Go home and eat and sleep and then
You'll rise up with the morning sun,
To build a Castle once again".

PEARLS

Pearls of wisdom do I pluck
From here and there and all around.
I take and study well their form,
And only keep those that are sound.

Bitter sweet, delight and pain,
All threaded through with smiles and tears.
I wear them humbly yet with pride,
To complement advancing years.

PRICE OF FREEDOM

On childhood we did reminisce
As through the grass we walked.
Of daisy chains and buttercups
And sunny days we talked.
And like that little girl I was,
I did discard my shoes
And jigged and hopped and danced around
My partner to amuse.
Till higher and higher and higher I leapt
And screamed, not in delight:
A clover bee had been disturbed
And clung to me in fright.
I sighed and said, as he sucked poison
From my adult toe,
"That's why in childhood in bare feet
We're not allowed to go".
He answered then with gravity,
"It really is quite plain,
That each fain step to freedom
Is accompanied by pain".

GHOST DANCERS AT RIBBLE HEAD

At Ribble Head on starry nights,
Just where the road curves round the stream,
A grassy bank a stage becomes,
Silver lighted with moonbeam.

Hush and you can hear the rushes
Whispering a soft refrain,
Teasing water on the pebbles,
Gently adding to the strain.

Now two lighted shadows enter,
Main performers in the theme;
Grace and rhythm, perfect union,
Vision of a bygone dream.

But the winds which sweep the moor know
That the ghosts were once complete;
Once had flesh and laughing eyes,
Caressing hands and dancing feet.

Now though cruel fate has deemed
Divergent paths their feet will tread,
Two souls which know no bounds but love
Defiant dance at Ribble Head.

ELLIOTT

You melt me with that weel' kent smile
And make my heart so glad,
But wheest, I willna tell your Mum —
You look just like your Dad!

Your sturdy back and haughty look
And independent gait
Accord a silent wisdom as
The world you contemplate.

And then so sweet and innocent
In vuln'rable repose:
In me a tide of primal raw
Emotions you expose.

I feel for your protection that
An army I could face,
And wish that I could make the world
For you a better place.

But chiefly with your rougin' eyes
Your Granny's heart you've won.
But wheest, I willna tell your Mum —
You are your Daddy's son!

TO RACHEL

I've danced on the moors beneath a silver moon,
I've danced with the poppies in a meadow in June,
I've danced with my lover through a summer storm,
And I've danced on the dew on a May Day morn.

But then as one grows older it usually is the case
That to dance in gay abandon you must choose a secret
    place,
For in public, with decorum you're expected to behave:
Childhood is for laughter: maturity is grave.

But last week quite spontaneously I took my grandchild's
    hand
And we danced right through a shopping street as folks
    around did stand
And with fond indulgent smiles, quite accepting, met the
    sight
Of the comic dancing duo of the mighty and the mite.

And so my little granddaughter has opened up a door
And I'm grateful to her that I can go dancing ever more.

MESSENGER OF HOPE

The February sun was pale,
The buildings gray and grim.
The figures swathed in furs and tweeds
Still shivered deep within.

The traffic sprayed the melting snow
And no one seemed to care;
The city was a hostile place,
My first year working there.

A corner then I rounded and
I found to my surprise,
A woman snugly sitting there
All smiling with her eyes,

With tiny snowdrops, beckoned me:
"Come, buy my flowers, I pray".
"I'll take them for my Mum", I said,
"Her birthday is today".

The winter warmed, I smiled and chose
The still white edge of snow,
To make my homeward journey
With a new found inner glow.

This set a pattern through the years;
As February came round
I always bought my mother
The first snowdrops that I found.

She was just like these tiny flowers;
No gaudy bloom was she,
But straight and true and full of hope:
She gave such strength to me.

I miss her now at snowdrop time,
Yet I am always glad
As I'm again reminded of
The special Mum I had.

"This world is full of care and woe,
I won't mind to be gone;
But it's the journey there I wish
I need not make alone".

I looked into her pain filled eyes
And all that I could see
Was my own little sister that
I'd had since I was three.

Her sparky wit was vital.
She was bonnier than me.
We'd shared so much together all
The time since I was three.

So off we set together on
Those last few daunting miles,
Each with our own sad burden,
Yet sharing tears and smiles.

We recollected memories
Of happy times now gone,
Of all the love and fun we'd had
From Mum and Dad at home.

And in the kinder evening light
Her face would lose its pain,
The vulnerable younger child
I'd known would come again.

Her husband and her family
Would join us on the way.
We'd laugh and talk, they'd come and go;
But not far would I stray.

The parting of the ways drew near,
I asked if she would be
Upon the other side when my
Turn came to wait for me.

I said, "Dear Sister, I have come
This far but can no further.
Please take these snowdrops home with you
And give my love to Mother".

*   *   *   *   *

Muriel died in March 1988 aged 51 years young at the Southern General Hospital, Govan, where she had worked for many years. I would like to express my gratitude and thanks to her friends in the Department of Obstetrics and Gynaecology and the staff in Ward 40 for their care and devotion; and to them and her family for allowing me to be with Muriel during the last stages of her illness.